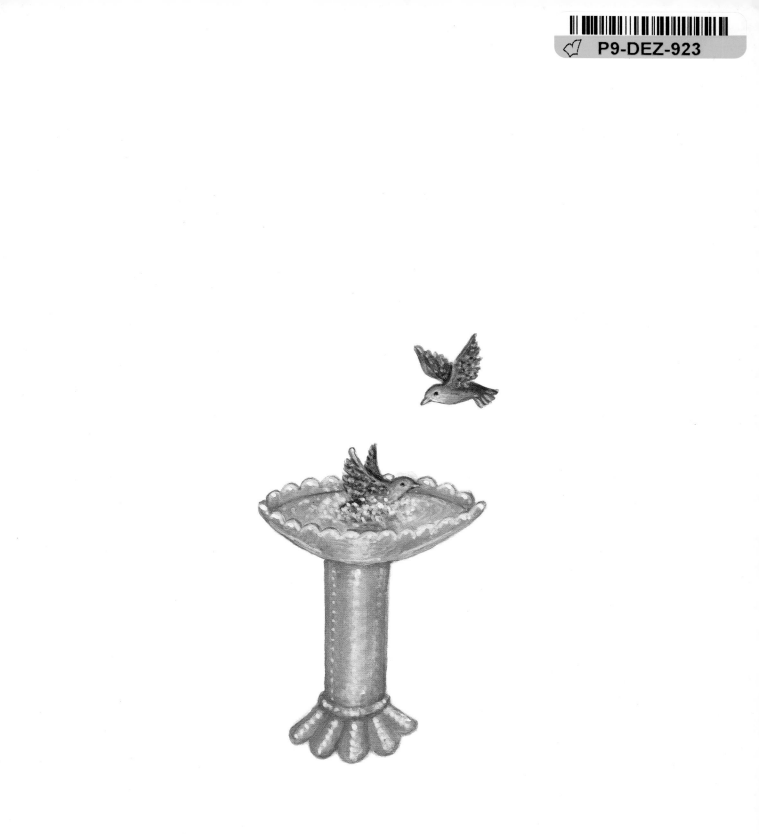

To my water babies, Cali, Cici, Caroline, Charlotte, Ana, and Alexander, with love. ~MB

For Lorna and Dave, with much love. ~SM

A warm thank you to publisher Karen Boersma and to editor Jennifer Stokes for their guidance. A special thank you to Susan Mitchell for her engaging, lively, and whimsical illustrations and to Claudia Dávila for her creative design work. ~MB

Text © 2014 Marilyn Baillie
Illustrations © 2014 Susan Mitchell

This paperback edition was originally published in 2014 for The Learning Partnership. Reprinted in 2015 and 2016. Not for resale.

Owlkids Books acknowledges the financial support of the Canada Council for the Arts, the Ontario Arts Council, the Government of Canada through the Canada Book Fund (CBF) and the Government of Ontario through the Ontario Media Development Corporation's Book Initiative for our publishing activities.

Published in Canada by
Owlkids Books Inc.
10 Lower Spadina Avenue
Toronto, ON M5V 2Z2

Published in the United States by
Owlkids Books Inc.
1700 Fourth Street
Berkeley, CA 94710

Library and Archives Canada Cataloguing in Publication

Baillie, Marilyn, author
    Whoosh! : a watery world of wonderful creatures / by Marilyn Baillie ; illustrated by Susan Mitchell.

ISBN 978-1-926973-98-2 (bound).--ISBN 978-1-771471-28-2 (pbk.)

    1. Aquatic animals--Juvenile literature. 2. Marine animals-- Juvenile literature. 3. Animal behavior--Juvenile literature.   I. Mitchell, Susan, 1962-, illustrator II. Title.

QL120.B35 2014   j591.76   C2013-904521-X

Edited by: Jennifer Stokes
Designed by: Claudia Dávila

Manufactured in Dongguan, China, in July 2016, by Toppan Leefung Packaging & Printing (Dongguan) Co., Ltd.
Job #BAYDC28

D   E   F   G   H

 Publisher of Chirp, chickaDEE and OWL
www.owlkidsbooks.com

Whoosh!

A watery world of wonderful creatures

Written by
Marilyn Baillie

Illustrated by
Susan Mitchell

Owl
kids

When you SWIM in the sea or SPLASH
in your bath, do you wonder what water
creature you'd like to be? Turn the page
to see which amazing animals love water,
just like you.

I am a playful dolphin, leaping high out of the sea.
I use my dolphin talk to keep in touch with my friends.
SQUEAK, WHISTLE, CLICK! CLICK! CLICK!

I am a water strider, but guess why I'm called the magic bug? I can race across lakes and ponds—my light body and long legs help me walk on water. Doesn't that seem like magic?

SHHH! I'm a great blue heron fishing for my supper. Silently, I keep watch through the ripples. SPLASH! In a flash, my long, strong beak catches a wriggling fish. SLURP! I swallow it whole.

I'm a tired alligator, cruising and keeping cool in the river. When it's time for my nap, I flop onto the rocks and snooze the day away. *ZZZZZZ!*

I'm a river otter pup. My mom pulls me into the chilly water for my first swimming lesson. Patiently, she teaches me to paddle and dive. Look at me float!

I am an orca whale swimming up for air. When I breathe out through my blowhole, I send up a fountain of spray! WHOOOSH!

I am a hermit crab hunting for a home. On the sandy seabed, I slip into an empty shell and settle down to stay. Mmmmm, it feels just right!

I'm a baby elephant having a bath with my mom. It's been a long, hot walk to our favourite watering hole. SWOOSH! That's cool! Spray me some more!

I'm a clownfish, and I stay safe in the sea anemone's stinging tentacles. I flutter about and look out from my wavy hiding spot. Peek-a-boo!

I am not just any penguin. I'm an Emperor Penguin! When I go fishing with my friends, we love to slide on our sleek bellies and dive into the sea. WHEE!

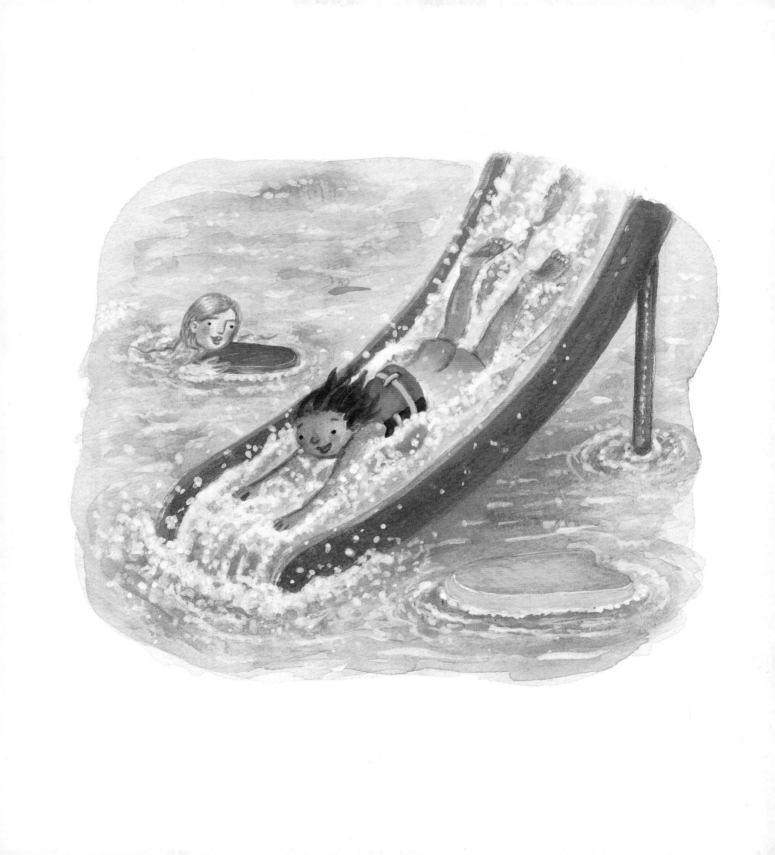

I bet you can't guess that I am a shark—a Tasseled Wobbegong shark! I fool these fish, too, with my seaweed disguise. Still as a stone, I wait and wait at the bottom of the reef...then CHOMP! I catch my dinner!

WATER IS PRECIOUS...
to you, to me, to all living things!

Can you think of ways
that you use water?

Did You Know?

Bottlenose Dolphin

With their noisy chatter, dolphins send out sound waves to gather news about what is swimming nearby. Their "dolphin talk" can even help them organize a fish hunt!

Great Blue Heron

At his nest, the heron opens his large beak for the chicks to reach inside. The fish that the heron has swallowed comes back up, mushy like baby food, ready for the chicks to eat.

Water Strider

How is the water strider able to "walk" on water? The secret is mainly in its long legs. Air is trapped under tiny hairs along the strider's legs. This air helps to hold the water strider up on water.

American Alligator

When an alligator needs to warm up, it lumbers onto the rocks to sleep in the sun. This way, it keeps its body temperature just right.

River Otter

One at a time, the mother otter teaches her pups to swim, float, and dive. After their lesson, she shows them how to dry off and keep warm.

Orca Whale

The orca whale closes up its blowhole when it swims under water. As the whale comes up to breathe, muscles open the hole and —*WHOOSH*— the whale blows out!

African Elephant

Elephants love all sorts of baths. Besides a water bath, they will give themselves a dust bath — or even roll in the mud for a mud bath!

Emperor Penguin

Emperor Penguins waddle and slide on land, but they are expert swimmers and divers in the sea. Their streamlined bodies cut through water, helping them catch fish or swerve out of danger.

Hermit Crab

Hermit crabs are fussy about their mobile homes. They often choose a dog whelk or periwinkle shell to live in. If two hermit crabs want the same shell, they fight for it!

Clownfish

Why are clownfish not poisoned by the sea anemone's sting? A coating of mucus on their skin protects them.

Tasseled Wobbegong Shark

With their pancake flat bodies and seaweed-like cover, Wobbegong sharks look like the sandy seabed. They are also surprisingly flexible and can squeeze into small caves to hide out and hunt.

Jump in the WATER and Join the Fun!

Scrunch way down and scuttle sideways like a  .

Soar high into the sky like a  leaping from the

waves. Now you are a  waddling on crunchy

ice. Flip flop your feet and dive deep, deep down to

fish in the sea. Are you a baby  splashing in

your bath? Or are you a fluttering  searching

for a secret hiding spot?

JUMP right in and see what wonderful
water creature you can be. SPLISH, SPLASH!